I Am Responsible/ Soy responsable

By Walt National   Traducción al español: Eduardo Alamán

Gareth Stevens
Publishing

Please visit our Web site, www.garethstevens.com. For a free color catalog of all our high-quality books, call toll free 1-800-542-2595 or fax 1-877-542-2596.

Cataloging Data

National, Walt.
 I am responsible / Soy responsable.
     p. cm. — (Kids of character / Chicos con carácter)
 Includes bibliographical references and index.
 ISBN 978-1-4339–4883-1 (library binding)
 1. Responsibility–Juvenile literature. I. Title.
 BJ1451.N38 2011
 179'.9–dc22
                                                          2010036898

First Edition

Published in 2011 by
Gareth Stevens Publishing
111 East 14th Street, Suite 349
New York, NY 10003

Copyright © 2011 Gareth Stevens Publishing

Editor: Mary Ann Hoffman
Designer: Christopher Logan
Spanish Translation: Eduardo Alamán

Photo credits: Cover, pp. 7, 9, 11, 13 Shutterstock.com; p. 1 Comstock/Thinkstock; p. 5 Ryan McVay/Photodisc/Thinkstock; p. 15 BananaStock/Thinkstock; p. 17 iStockphoto.com; p. 19 iStockphoto/Thinkstock; p. 21 Tim Kitchen/The Image Bank/ Getty Images.

Printed in the United States of America

CPSIA compliance information: Batch #CW11GS: For further information contact Gareth Stevens, New York, New York at 1-800-542-2595.

Table of Contents

Contenido

Boldface words appear in the glossary/
Las palabras en **negrita** aparecen en el glosario

A Responsible Person

A responsible person does their job without being told. They keep their word. A responsible person does the right thing. A responsible person can be trusted.

- -

Una persona responsable

Una persona responsable hace su trabajo sin que se lo digan. Las personas responsables cumplen su palabra. Además hacen lo correcto. Una persona responsable es una persona confiable.

In the Neighborhood

Marco's neighbor went on a trip. He asked Marco to pick up his mail. Each day, Marco watched for the mailman. Then he went and got his neighbor's mail. Marco is responsible.

En el barrio

El vecino de Marco salió de viaje y le pidió a Marco que recogiera su correo. Todos los días Marco esperó al cartero. Luego fue a recoger el correo. Marco es responsable.

Betty said she would plant trees in her neighborhood on Saturday. Betty's friend asked her to go to the movies instead. Betty said she couldn't go. She worked in the neighborhood. Betty is responsible.

- -

Betty dijo que plantaría árboles en su vecindario el sábado. Un amigo la invitó al cine. Betty le dijo que no podía ir y se quedó a trabajar en su vecindario. Betty es responsable.

At School

Jack had homework to finish. His friends asked him to go to the park. Jack said he could go after he finished his homework. Jack is responsible.

En la escuela

Jack tenía que terminar su tarea. Sus amigos lo invitaron al parque. Jack les dijo que iría al acabar su tarea. Jack es responsable.

The children were on the school playground. Danny saw that the slide was broken. She told the teacher. Danny is responsible.

Los chicos estaban jugando en el patio de la escuela. Danny vio que el tobogán estaba roto. Danny se lo dijo a la maestra. Danny es responsable.

The teacher asked Ben to make sure there were enough crayons in the art center every day. Each morning, Ben checked the crayons without being told. Ben is responsible.

- -

La maestra le encargó un trabajo a Ben. Todos los días, Ben tenía que revisar que hubiese suficientes crayolas en el cuarto de arte. Sin que nadie le dijera, Ben revisaba cada mañana si había suficientes crayolas. Ben es responsable.

At Home

Joe's job was to take out the **garbage** each night after dinner. One night, Joe wanted to watch a TV show after dinner. He took out the garbage first. Joe is responsible.

En casa

El trabajo de Joe es sacar la **basura** todos los días después de cenar. Una noche, Joe quería ver la televisión después de cenar. Joe sacó la basura primero. Joe es responsable.

Sara's mother told her to come home from her friend's house before it got dark. Sara and her friend were playing a game. Sara didn't finish the game. She went home before it got dark. Sara is responsible.

La mamá de Sara le dijo que regresara a casa antes de que anocheciera. Sara estaba jugando en casa de una amiga. Sara y su amiga jugaban un juego de mesa. Sara no terminó el juego y regresó a casa antes del anochecer. Sara es responsable.

Billy got a new bike. His parents told him to wear a **helmet**. They said it would **protect** him if he fell. Billy wore his helmet when he rode his bike. Billy is responsible.

- -

Billy tiene una bicicleta nueva. Sus papás le dijeron que tenía que usar un **casco**. El casco es una **protección** en caso de que Billy se caiga. Billy siempre usa el casco cuando anda en su bicicleta. Billy es responsable.

Glossary/Glosario

garbage: waste or trash

helmet: a hard covering that keeps your head safe

protect: to keep safe

- -

basura (la) sobras o desperdicios

casco (el) una cubierta, sólida, que mantiene la cabeza segura

proteger mantener a alguien seguro

For More Information/Más información

Books/Libros

Glassman, Bruce. *Responsibility*. San Diego, CA: Bearing Books, 2008.

Lehman, Dana. *I DOUBLE Dare You!* Allenton, MI: Lehman Publishing, 2008.

Web Sites/Páginas en Internet

Being Responsible Shows Character
www.school-for-champions.com/character/responsible.htm
Read how being responsible can help you in your life.

Exercising Character: Responsibility
charactercounts.org/pdf/Exercising-Character/Exer-Char_06-09-responsibility.pdf
Find activities on how to be responsible.

Index/Índice